CAMPING

OUTDOOR ADVENTURES

DAVID ARMENTROUT

D1716134

The Rourke Press, Inc.
Vero Beach, Florida 32964

David Armentrout specializes in nonfiction writing and has had several book series published for primary schools. He resides in Cincinnati with his wife and two children.

PHOTO CREDITS
©Gordon Wiltsie: cover, page 19; East Coast Studios: pages 4, 7, 9, 10, 13, 15, 18; © Ace Kvale: pages 6, 22; © George Ancona/International Stock: page 12; © Dusty Willison/International Stock: page 16; © Buddy Mays/International Stock: page 21

EDITORIAL SERVICES:
Penworthy Learning Systems

Library of Congress Cataloging-in-Publication Data

Armentrout, David, 1962-
    Camping / David Armentrout.
        p. cm. — (Outdoor adventures)
    Includes bibliographical references (p.24) and index.
    Summary: Discusses the popularity and different kinds of camping and covers such aspects as supplies, equipment, setting up, cooking, and safety factors.
    ISBN 1-57103-202-9
    1. Camping—Juvenile literature. [1. Camping.] I. Title II. Series:
Armentrout, David. 1962- Outdoor adventures.
GV191.7.A746 1998
796.54—dc21   98–18417
                                                              CIP
                                                               AC

Printed in the USA

TABLE OF CONTENTS

CAMPING

Camping is living outdoors for a short time. People camp for many reasons, but the most common reason is to get away and enjoy nature.

Camping is a great outdoor activity because it can be done any time of the year. National and state parks are popular places to camp, and most parks have areas called campgrounds. Parks also have hiking trails, historic places, and lakes or rivers for fishing and boating.

Campers usually use a tent or a **recreational vehicle** (REK ree AY shun ul VEE i kul), or RV, to sleep in. Some campers like the night air and sleep under the stars.

If the weather is hot, try to choose a campsite with shady trees.

DIFFERENT WAYS TO CAMP

There are different ways to camp. **Primitive** (PRIM i tiv) camping is the simplest form of camping. There are no modern **facilities** (fuh SIL i teez) like toilets and showers. There is also no fresh running water.

This boy camps where he can also fish.

Some campers have toilets, water, and electricity, just like home.

Full-service camping offers many of the comforts of home. Most full-service campgrounds have toilets, showers, electric hook-ups, cabins or other shelters, and even a small store.

Some campgrounds have only a few modern comforts. These camping areas may have a water pump and toilets but may not have showers, a store, or electricity.

WHERE TO CAMP

Planning a camping trip can be as much fun as the trip itself. There are thousands of camping areas in the United States alone. The National Park Service, the Boy Scouts and Girl Scouts of America, and state **tourism** (TOOR IZ um) departments have facts about camping areas. Road maps, travel guides, and magazines can also help you decide on a great camping spot.

Once you've picked a place to camp, call the campground or park service to see if you need a reservation or camping permit. Most camping areas charge a fee to stay overnight. You should also ask if campfires and pets are allowed.

This camper uses a miniature stove to cook a hot meal.

CAMPING SUPPLIES

Basic camping supplies include a tent, sleeping bag, cooking stove, and flashlight. Most campers also take along a light and an ax to chop wood. If you plan to hike to a campsite, you will need a backpack to hold your supplies.

Playing and having fun is what camping is all about. Bring plenty of things to play with. When your day of hiking or fishing is over, you can have a game of catch or horseshoes. A deck of cards or a board game comes in handy after the sun goes down.

Don't forget to pack a camera and film. Pictures are a great way to share and remember your camping experience.

If you plan to camp in the woods, you must carry everything you will need.

SETTING UP CAMP

Setting up camp can go smoothly if everyone pitches in. First unpack the gear and set up the tent if you will be sleeping in one. Sleeping bags and clothing can be stored in the tent. If you are camping close to your car, you can keep food inside the car until it is time to prepare it.

Everyone should help set up camp.

These campers have less to set up than people who camp in tents.

RV campers may need to unload a few articles and set up a screen tent or other small shelter. Their sleeping area and cooking stove are inside the RV.

People who camp under the stars can unpack supplies and gather firewood.

LOW IMPACT CAMPING

Low impact (LO IM PAKT) camping means changing as little as possible in the area where you camp. Follow these helpful hints to be a low impact camper.

Use a camping area that has been used before. Use campfire rings and be sure to completely put out any fire before going to sleep or leaving the campsite.

Do not destroy any plants or trees. Use only fallen logs and limbs for firewood.

Remember water is important to all living things. Do not wash or dump anything in natural springs or rivers. Do not litter. Take all trash with you when you leave.

These campers in the high mountains leave nothing behind when they leave.

CAMPFIRE COOKING

What do you eat when camping? Primitive campers sometimes bring small gas stoves and prepare hot meals. **Freeze-dried** (FREEZ-DRYD) food is lightweight, takes up little space, and cooks quickly. All you do is add boiling water, stir, and wait.

Some campers use larger camp stoves with two or three burners. Many things that you cook at home can be prepared on a camp stove.

Some campers enjoy campfire cooking. The hot coals of a wood fire will cook hot dogs, steaks, fresh fish, potatoes, baked beans, and hot drinks.

A campfire can be used for cooking and keeping warm.

CAMPING AND COMMON SENSE

Campers must use common sense. The natural areas you camp in are home to many wild animals. Since animals are drawn to food, you must store food in your car or tie it in a box high in a tree.

Never play with campfire.

You can use campfire to cook a hot breakfast.

Besides sharing your space with animals, you may have camping neighbors. Always respect other campers' space and privacy, and remember no one likes loud campers.

Campfires are a major cause of forest fires. Never leave a fire unattended. Make sure there is plenty of water, dirt, or sand to put out the fire.

SAFETY AND FIRST AID

Safety is always a concern when on a camping trip. Some campsites are close to a river's edge or a cliffside, or there may be loose dirt and rocks on nearby trails. Other concerns are muddy or icy areas. Simply watching where you walk can prevent falls, scrapes, and cuts.

Another concern is wild animals. Be sure to keep your distance when looking at wildlife. Don't take risks by getting too close to animals when trying to take a picture.

Take a first-aid kit with the right supplies. You may need to clean and cover a cut, remove a splinter, or care for insect bites or poison oak or ivy.

Some wild animals can be dangerous. This moose could attack at any time.

GLOSSARY

facilities (fuh SIL i teez) — something that makes life or work easier, more pleasant

freeze-dried (FREEZ-DRYD) — dried while frozen to preserve freshness

low impact (LO IM PAKT) — having little or no effect on

primitive (PRIM i tiv) — in the simplest or most basic form

recreational vehicle (REK ree AY shun ul VEE i kul), or RV — a truck and camper combined that has a built-in kitchen (sink, stove, and so on)

tourism (TOOR IZ um) — traveling for pleasure; the business of providing tours and services for travelers

Take a book or game to keep you busy when you are camping.

INDEX

FURTHER READING

Find out more about Outdoor Adventures with these helpful books and information sites:

McManners, Hugh. *The Outdoor Adventure Handbook.* DK Publishing, 1996.

Logue, Victoria; Logue, Frank; and Carroll, Mark. *Kids Outdoors/Skills and Knowledge for Outdoor Adventures.* Ragged Mountain Press, 1996.

DuFresne, Jim. *Outdoor Adventures With Children.* The Mountaineers, 1990.

Hodgson, Michael. *Wilderness With Children/A Parents Guide to Fun Family Outings.* Stackpole Books, 1992.

Greenspan, Rick and Kahn, Hal. *The Camper's Companion.* Foghorn Press, 1993.

Internet address for the National Park Foundation:
   www.nationalparks.org/guide/us_map.htm